OUTSTANDING AFRICAN AMERICANS

GREAT AFRICAN AMERICANS IN
BUSINESS

PAT REDIGER

Crabtree Publishing Company

Dedication

This series is dedicated to the African-American men and women who dared to follow their dreams. With courage, faith, and hard work, they overcame obstacles in their lives and went on to excel in their fields. They fought for civil rights and encouraged hope and self-reliance. They celebrated the glory of the athlete and the joy of knowledge and learning. They brought entertainment, poetry, and song to the world, and we are richer for it. *Outstanding African Americans* is both an acknowledgement of and a tribute to these people.

Project Manager
Amanda Woodrow

Writing Team
Karen Dudley
Pat Rediger

Editor
Virginia Mainprize

Research
Karen Dudley

Design and layout
Warren Clark
Karen Dudley

Photograph Credits
Archive Photos: page 40 (Shooting Star); **Reuters/Bettman:** page 18; **UPI/Bettman:** pages 21, 42; **Birmingham News Company:** pages 6-9; **Canapress Photo Service:** pages 5, 13, 22, 27, 44; **Dr. A.G. Gaston:** page 4; **E.G. Bowman Company:** page 52; *Essence*: page 58; **Gardner & Proctor Advertising:** page 55; **Madame C.J. Walker Collection, Indiana Historical Society Library:** pages 38, 39; **Naomi Sims:** pages 28-30, 32, 33; **Ponopresse Internationale Inc.:** pages 11, 12, 15, 16, 19, 20, 41; **Retna Ltd.:** pages 10 (Marzullo), 14 (Gray), 43, 45 (McBride), 46 (Granitz), 49 (Buckmaster); **Schomburg Center for Research in Black Culture, The New York Public Library, Astor, Lenox and Tilden Foundations:** pages 23-26, 31, 34-37, 61.

Published by
Crabtree Publishing Company

350 Fifth Avenue,	360 York Road, R.R. 4	73 Lime Walk
Suite 3308	Niagara-on-the-Lake,	Headington
New York, New York	Ontario Canada	Oxford Ox3 7AD
U.S.A. 10018	L0S 1J0	United Kingdom

Cataloging-in-Publication Data

Rediger, Pat, 1966-
Great African Americans in business/by Pat Rediger.
   p. cm. —(Outstanding African Americans series)
Includes index
Summary: Examines the lives of more than ten African American men and women, including Oprah Winfrey, Don Cornelius, and Naomi Sims, with the obstacles they each overcame.
   ISBN 0-86505-803-2 (lib. bdg.)—ISBN 0-8605-817-2 (pbk.)
1. Afro-Americans in business—Biography—Juvenile literature. [1. Businessmen. 2. Businesswomen. 3. Afro Americans—Biography.] I. Title. II. Series: Rediger, Pat, 1966- Outstanding African Americans series.
   HC102.5.A2R36 1995   95-24879
   338'.0089'96073—dc20   CIP
   [B]   AC

Contents

Arthur Gaston

Personality Profile

Career: Business executive and founder of many successful companies.

Born: July 4, 1892, in Demopolis, Alabama.

Family: Married Creola Smith, date unknown, (died, 1938); married Minnie, 1939. Has one son, Arthur George, Jr. (deceased).

Education: Grade ten certificate at the Tuggle Institute.

Awards: National Award of Achievement, U.S. Department of Commerce, 1972; *Black Enterprise* Achievement award, 1978; *Black Enterprise* Entrepreneur of the Century award, 1992; numerous honorary degrees.

Growing Up

Arthur was born in 1892 in the log cabin his grandparents had built in Demopolis, Alabama. Arthur's grandparents had been slaves before the Emancipation Proclamation of 1863 made slavery illegal. But freedom did not mean a better life for most African Americans. Soon after Arthur was born, his father died, and his mother had to work as a domestic servant to make ends meet.

Arthur was eight years old when his mother got a job as a cook, and they moved to Birmingham, Alabama. Arthur enrolled at the Tuggle Institute, a black school. Here he heard a speech by Booker T. Washington, a famous African-American educator. Booker told the students that education and success in business were the ways to overcome their poverty and social conditions. Arthur was inspired.

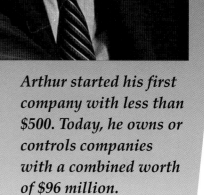

Arthur started his first company with less than $500. Today, he owns or controls companies with a combined worth of $96 million.

After he left school, Arthur sold subscriptions to the *Birmingham Reporter*, a black newspaper. Later he worked as a bellhop at the Battle House Hotel in Mobile, Alabama. He made so much money at the hotel that when he was offered a job at the post office, Arthur turned it down.

When World War I began, Arthur enlisted in the army and was sent to France with an all-black unit. He served with distinction and came home from the war determined to succeed in life.

Developing Skills

Arthur in front of the Citizens Federal Savings and Loan Association which he founded in 1957.

Even as a young child, Arthur showed a talent for business. Whenever the neighborhood children came to his yard, he charged them a button or pin to play on his swing. Then he sold the buttons and pins to his neighbors. As Arthur grew up, his business flair developed and grew.

When World War I ended, Arthur returned to Birmingham and got a job as a laborer at the Tennessee Coal and Iron Company. He was paid $3.10 a day, a good wage for those times, but Arthur found other ways to make money. He asked his mother to prepare boxed lunches which he sold to his fellow workers. He also started selling popcorn and peanuts. Arthur was able to save most of his paychecks, and he began to lend money to his co-workers. He charged them twenty-five cents interest for two weeks on every dollar, and they had to pay him back on their next pay day. His savings began to grow fast.

Arthur noticed that many black workers died without having enough money to pay for their funerals. Whenever someone came to the factory asking for donations for a burial, people would always chip in. However, sometimes dishonest people would come collecting for people who were still alive. Arthur decided to form the Booker T. Washington Burial Society to organize and collect insurance money for funerals.

In the beginning, not many people were willing to join the society. When the first member died, the company was short seventy dollars for her funeral. Success came when the preacher from the Hopewell Baptist Church urged his congregation to support Arthur. By 1930, the company had become so successful that Arthur and his father-in-law opened a funeral home and started Smith and Gaston Funeral Directors.

Arthur with some of the many awards he has received.

Arthur began to build his business empire. He founded a business college for African Americans, a real estate and investment company, and a motel. When he was in his seventies, he opened the A. G. Gaston Home for Senior Citizens; when he was in his eighties, he bought two radio stations. At ninety-four, he founded a construction company. Even when he was 100 years old, Arthur still went into the office every day.

Accomplishments

1923 Founded the Booker T. Washington Burial Society.	**1955** Founded the Vulcan Realty and Investment Company.
1932 Founded Smith and Gaston Funeral Directors.	**1957** Founded the Citizens Federal Savings and Loan Association.
1939 Founded the Booker T. Washington Business College.	**1963** Founded the A.G. Gaston Home for Senior Citizens.
1946 Founded the Brown Belle Bottling Company.	**1975** Acquired the radio stations WENN and WAGG.
1954 Founded the A.G. Gaston Motel.	**1986** Founded the A.G. Gaston Construction Company.

Overcoming Obstacles

At an early age, Arthur became aware of racism when a young man in his town was lynched because he did not get off the sidewalk for a white woman. Arthur himself experienced racism when he joined the army and was forced to serve in a segregated unit. Although Arthur and many other black soldiers served with distinction in the war, when they returned to the United States, they found themselves treated with disrespect and hostility because of their color.

"The one thing that [Martin Luther King, Jr.] and I differed on [was that] I always felt that if somebody hit me, I would have to hit them back."

Arthur poses in front of the A.G. Gaston Motel in Birmingham, Alabama.

Arthur was determined to overcome racism by succeeding in business. His slogan was "Find a need and fill it." When he saw that many white businesses refused to serve black customers, he realized that he had found the perfect business opportunity. Arthur set out to build his empire by founding companies especially for African Americans.

When Arthur had trouble finding enough black office workers to staff his companies, he followed his motto and founded the Booker T. Washington Business College. Under the administration of Arthur's wife, Minnie, the college trained African Americans to operate business machines.

Because African Americans were not welcome in Birmingham motels, Arthur opened the A.G. Gaston Motel in 1954 to accommodate them. When he saw that most banks refused to lend money to African Americans, he founded his own bank, the Citizens Federal Savings and Loan Association, so black people could borrow money to build homes and churches.

As news of Arthur's wealth spread, he was the victim of an attempted kidnapping. The kidnappers hit him on the head with a hammer, handcuffed him, and drove him around Birmingham for hours before being caught by the police.

Arthur based his success on his motto, "Find a need and fill it."

Although Arthur made his fortune serving African Americans, he was criticized by the black community for refusing to take part in the nonviolent civil rights demonstrations of the 1960s. Arthur felt that if someone pushed him, he would have to fight back. However, he was active behind the scenes, working hard to convince white businesses to give equal treatment to African Americans. Despite bomb threats by white racists, he allowed civil rights leaders to stay in his motel for free. He also provided the bail money for many of the protesters who had been jailed, including Martin Luther King, Jr. As Arthur said later, "*Somebody* had to be able to get them out of jail."

Special Interests

- Arthur believes in helping young people. In the 1960s, he established the A.G. Gaston Boys and Girls Club for city children. He often visits the club to talk to the children and motivate them with his success story.
- Arthur's favorite businesses are the gospel and the rhythm and blues radio stations that he purchased in 1975.
- Always appreciative of his staff, Arthur sold the Booker T. Washington Insurance Company to them in 1987 at a fraction of its estimated value.

Berry Gordy, Jr.

Personality Profile

Career: Business executive, producer, and composer.

Born: November 28, 1929, in Detroit, Michigan, to Berry, Sr. and Bertha Gordy.

Family: Married Thelma Coleman, 1953, (divorced, 1959); married Raynoma Liles, (divorced, 1962); married Grace Eaton, 1990. Has six children, Hazel Joy, Berry IV, Terry, Kerry, Kennedy, and Stefan.

Education: Received high-school diploma while serving in the army.

Awards: Business Achievement Award, Interracial Council for Business Opportunity, 1967; Second Annual American Music Award for Outstanding Contribution to Industry, 1975; One of Five Leading Entrepreneurs of the Nation, Babson College, 1978; Whitney M. Young, Jr. Award, Los Angeles Urban League, 1980; elected Gordon Grand Fellow, Yale University, 1985; inducted into the Rock and Roll Hall of Fame, 1988.

Growing Up

Berry grew up in a supportive, successful family. His father was a plastering contractor, and his mother was an insurance agent. They also ran a grocery store and print shop. After school, Berry worked in his parents' stores, and, during his spare time, he picked out tunes on the piano in their recreation room. But his first real love was boxing.

Berry lived near Joe Louis's neighborhood of Black Bottom in Detroit. Like most other African-American boys of that time, Berry dreamed of becoming a boxer like Joe. Back then, boxing was one of the few sports open to blacks, and training was cheap. Berry trained at the Detroit City Recreation Center. He was a good fighter and won most of his bouts. In 1948, he turned professional.

But Berry soon discovered that even the best fighters never made very much money. He quit fighting and, after spending two years in the army, opened a record store in Detroit.

The family put great emphasis on unity and support. At almost every fight, Berry's entire family was there cheering him on.

Berry speaking at the Songwriters Hall of Fame.

Developing Skills

Berry used his army savings and $700 that he borrowed from his family and opened the 3-D Record Mart in 1955. Although the store lasted less than a year, the experience taught Berry a lot about the music industry.

For a while, Berry worked on the assembly line at the Ford Motor Company and wrote songs in his spare time. Some of these songs were recorded by local singers, but Berry was often unhappy with the way his songs were produced. In 1957, he quit Ford to be a full-time songwriter, and, in 1958, he began working as an independent record producer.

Berry with Motown recording artist Stevie Wonder.

He recorded songs by the Miracles, Marv Johnson, and Eddie Holland and sent them to national record companies such as Chess, United Artists, and End. Still Berry was not happy with the way his songs were produced. He also disliked how little money he was paid by the big companies.

By the end of 1959, when Berry was just thirty years old, he established his own record company, Motown. It began with six people working in a small apartment and grew to be the largest independent record company in the world. It launched many famous singers such as the Supremes, the Jackson 5, and their youngest brother, Michael.

Throughout the 1960s, Motown continued to place hits on both the rhythm and blues and pop charts, and many of them reached Number One. Berry also wanted to get his songs in movies and to have his singers star in Hollywood films. So, in 1972, Motown moved from Detroit to Los Angeles.

Berry established Motown Industries in 1973. The new company handled records, motion pictures, television, and publishing. Some of the films released by Motown Industries include *Mahogany* (1975), *The Wiz* (1978), and *The Last Dragon* (1985).

In 1983, "Motown 25 — Yesterday, Today, and Forever" was shown on NBC-TV. The program featured all of Motown's singing stars. It was the most-watched variety show in television history and was nominated for nine Emmy awards.

In 1988, Berry sold Motown Records to MCA, Inc. for $61 million. He continues to run the Gordy Company which includes the film, television, and publishing divisions of Motown Industries. He is working on his autobiography.

In 1988, Berry was inducted into the Rock and Roll Hall of Fame.

Accomplishments

1951-53 Served with the U.S. Army.	**1973** Founded and became president of Motown Industries.
1955 Opened the 3-D Record Mart which closed soon afterwards.	**1988** Sold Motown Records to MCA, Inc. and became director of the Gordy Company.
1959 Founded Motown Record Corporation.	

Overcoming Obstacles

"[The Motown sound] is not just climbing up out of poverty, escaping from it – it's being young, creating, doing things with dignity. It's pride."

I t was no easy task taking a small company and turning it into a multimillion-dollar business. Without Berry, Motown would never have been such a success. But Berry was forced to make many unpopular decisions along the way. One of the toughest was Motown's move from Detroit to Los Angeles in 1972. Without the move, Berry knew that Motown would never grow to be a large corporation. Many of Berry's employees were upset because they did not want to leave their homes.

Many talented young singers were first attracted to the company because they liked the small family feeling at Motown. But as the company grew, Berry became less involved in the daily operations. Motown's other executives mistreated some singers who developed a deep hatred for Berry. Berry met this obstacle by explaining his side of the story in books, films, and television specials.

Berry autographs a copy of his book, **To Be Loved: The Music, The Magic, The Memories of Motown.**

14

Berry had problems with some of his film ventures. He was very successful with *Lady Sings the Blues*. It starred Diana Ross, who was nominated for an Academy Award for her performance in 1972. But both *Mahogany* and *The Wiz* were box-office flops and received bad reviews from the film critics. As the producer of both films, Berry took the criticism personally. It was not until 1985 that he produced another film, *The Last Dragon*. The movie was a kung-fu musical that did well at the box office.

Berry and his wife, Grace, at a reception honoring actor Sidney Poitier.

Special Interests

- Berry is very close to his family. He appointed his brothers and sisters to key executive positions in Motown. His second wife, Raynoma, was an early vice-president. He named his first publishing company Jobete after his first three children, Hazel Joy, Berry IV, and Terry.
- He organizes the Sterling Ball to assist inner-city students continue their studies. This annual charitable event has helped many students, both black and white, go to college.
- Berry has bought several large houses over the years. In 1965, he purchased the Gordy Manor in Detroit. In the early 1970s, he bought a mansion in Los Angeles from comedian Red Skelton.

John H. Johnson

Personality Profile

Career: Founder of the Johnson Publishing Company.

Born: January 19, 1918, in Arkansas City, Arkansas, to Leroy and Gertrude Johnson.

Family: Married Eunice Walker, 1941. Has two children, John (died, 1981) and Linda.

Education: DuSable High School, Chicago; University of Chicago; Northwestern School of Commerce.

Awards: Named one of 10 Outstanding Young Men of the Year, 1951, by the U.S. Junior Chamber of Commerce; Spingarn Medal, 1966; inductee, Chicago Business Hall of Fame, 1983; named Chicagoan of the Year, 1984; Jackie Robinson Award, 1985; Publishing Hall of Fame, 1987; Black Press Hall of Fame, 1987; Black Journalists' Lifetime Achievement Award, 1987; Entrepreneur of the Decade, *Black Enterprise*, 1987; numerous honorary degrees.

Growing Up

John was born in a tin-roofed house in Arkansas City in 1918. The family had to work hard to survive. John learned how to work before he learned how to play. He helped his mother wash clothes and cook meals for the laborers hired to build up the banks of the flooding Mississippi River.

John's mother was loving but strict, and she insisted that he get a good education. The only problem was that Arkansas City had no high school for blacks. John and his mother were determined that he continue his schooling, so they decided to move to Chicago where John could go to high school.

Even though they tried very hard, they could not save enough money to get to Chicago before the next school year started. John's mother did not want him to run wild on the streets, so she insisted that he repeat the eighth grade.

By the next school year, John and his mother had saved enough money to move to Chicago. John enrolled in high school and gained a reputation as an excellent student. He was elected junior and senior class president and graduated with honors.

"My mother never went beyond the third grade. Yet she was the best educated person I ever met....She believed you could do anything you wanted to do, if you tried. She gave me that faith and that hope, and that has guided my life."

Developing Skills

When John graduated from high school in 1936, he wanted to go to college. He had won a partial scholarship to the University of Chicago, but he still did not have enough money to attend. John was invited to a lunch to honor the best high-school students. The featured speaker was John's hero, Harry Pace, the president of the Supreme Liberty Life Insurance Company. After the speech, John met Harry who was so impressed with him that he offered John a part-time job as an office boy to help him through college.

John left university to work full-time at Supreme Life. One of his jobs was to find magazine articles about the black community. Because Harry was too busy to read the magazines himself, John had to take notes and tell Harry about the articles. John wondered if other people would be interested in the same kind of information.

From its humble beginnings, John built the Johnson Publishing Company into a financial empire.

John came up with the idea of a magazine for blacks called *Negro Digest*. But no bank would lend him the money to start, so he borrowed $500 from a small loan company and promised to give them all his mother's furniture if he could not pay back the money. John wrote to everyone on Supreme Life's mailing list asking them to subscribe to the digest. Three thousand people sent back their two-dollar subscription fee, and *Negro Digest* was born.

Inspired by his success, John began thinking about publishing a picture magazine like *Life* that would cover black news and people. He decided to call the magazine *Ebony*. In 1945, the first issue of *Ebony* was published, and all 25,000 copies sold out right away.

In 1950, John began publishing the women's magazine *Tan*, and, in 1951, he launched *Jet*. In 1962, John expanded his company and began publishing books.

Today, John heads the wealthiest black business in the United States. His wife, Eunice, is the secretary-treasurer of the company, and his daughter, Linda, is the president of Johnson Publishing.

John and his daughter, Linda, who is now the president of Johnson Publishing.

Accomplishments

1936 Began part-time work at the Supreme Liberty Life Insurance Company.

1942 The first issue of *Negro Digest* was published.

1945 The first issue of *Ebony* was published.

1950 Started *Tan* and *Hue* magazines which later failed.

1951 Launched *Jet* magazine, a weekly newsmagazine which has a strong following today.

1962 The Johnson Publishing Company published its first book, *Burn, Killer, Burn.*

1985 The first issue of *Ebony Man* was published.

Overcoming Obstacles

When John and his mother moved to Chicago, they had very little money. The other children used to make fun of John for his country accent and homemade clothes. John was hurt by their teasing, but he decided to get back at them by beating them in high grades. He started to study harder and speak out in class. Before long he earned the respect of his classmates.

When John wanted to publish *Negro Digest*, he found that he also had to earn the respect of the banks. He tried to borrow the money to start the magazine, but every bank turned him down. An assistant in the First National Bank of Chicago laughed in his face. Today John is a special customer at that bank and can borrow as much money as he wants.

Although every bank turned him down, John found a small company that would lend him the money. He used the money to send letters asking people to subscribe to his new magazine. When thousands of people sent in their subscription fee, John started the digest.

"I've been in the ditch, and I've been on the mountaintop, and, believe me, being on the mountaintop is better."

But John's problems did not end there. After *Negro Digest* was published, John found that many distributors did not want to carry it because they thought it would not sell. John had all his friends go to their local newsstands and ask for a copy. When a few stores started to stock the magazine, John paid his friends to buy all the copies so *Negro Digest* would sell out, and the distributors would see that it was popular.

Within six months, each issue was selling 50,000 copies. Then, when Eleanor Roosevelt, the wife of the president of the United States, wrote an article for the digest, sales jumped to 100,000 copies.

Despite the magazine's success, many companies did not want to advertise in it. They felt that it would be a waste of money because they believed that blacks were not rich enough to buy their products. In response, John created five mail-order companies which sold hair products, clothes, vitamins, and wigs. He advertised these products in *Negro Digest*.

In 1958, John decided to start the Ebony Fashion Show. Today it travels to almost 190 cities around the world. John also discovered that there were no cosmetics made especially for black women, so he founded the Fashion Fair Cosmetics Company, the largest black-owned cosmetics company in the world.

Special Interests

- John is active in the civil rights movement and has served on the board of directors of the Urban League since 1958.
- In his spare time, John likes to cook and shop for groceries.
- John has written his autobiography, *Succeeding against the Odds*.

Rose Morgan

Personality Profile

Career: Beautician and business executive.

Born: 1913, in Shelby, Mississippi, to Chaptle Morgan.

Family: Married Joe Louis, 1955, (marriage annulled, 1958); married Louis Saunders, (separated, two years later).

Education: Attended the Morris School of Beauty.

Awards: Outstanding Achievement Award, New York State Beauty Culturists Association.

Growing Up

R ose was born in Shelby, Mississippi, in 1913, but her father moved the family to Chicago, Illinois, when she was six years old. Throughout Rose's childhood her father, Chaptle, played a key role. He praised everything she did and always told her to strive for success. Because of her father's encouragement, Rose grew up believing that she could accomplish anything if she set her mind to it.

Chaptle had been a successful sharecropper, a farmer who works on someone else's land and is paid with a share of the crop. He believed in the importance of hard work, a lesson he taught Rose. Even as a child, she knew that she wanted to have her own business.

When Rose was just ten years old, her father helped her start her first business. She made artificial flowers and organized the neighborhood children to sell them door to door. Rose discovered that she had a talent for cutting hair. By the time she was fourteen, she was earning spending money by cutting and styling her friends' hair.

"I watched [my father] keep accounts all his life. Being in business for myself was always in my mind."

After she finished high school, Rose decided to expand her talents by attending the Morris School of Beauty. Here she learned a lot about beauty and hair styling. After she graduated, she rented a booth in a local beauty salon and began to take in clients on a full-time basis. As her satisfied customers spread the word about her talents, Rose's business grew.

R ose had her first big break in 1938 when she met singer Ethel Waters. Rose styled Ethel's hair for a performance, and Ethel was so impressed with Rose's talent that she invited Rose to travel with her to New York City.

Rose's hard work and determination helped build her business empire.

Rose was enchanted with the glamour of New York. With her father's approval, she moved to the city and started working as a beautician. Within six months, Rose had become such a success that she opened her own beauty salon in the converted kitchen of a friend's apartment. Business was so good that Rose hired and trained five assistants to help her.

Her business soon outgrew the small kitchen, so Rose and a friend signed a ten-year lease on an old mansion known as the Haunted House. The mansion had been empty for years and needed a lot of renovations. Many of Rose's friends thought she had made a mistake. But she set to the task with determination, and soon the Rose Meta House of Beauty was open for business. Within three years, the salon became the largest black-owned beauty shop in the country.

Rose continued to expand her business by developing her own line of cosmetics for African-American women. She also began organizing fashion shows which featured her employees and customers as well as professional models. These fashion shows quickly became popular social events drawing thousands of people to the Renaissance Casino in Harlem.

As her success grew, Rose traveled to Paris, France, the fashion capital of the world. There she promoted her products and demonstrated her beauty techniques on black women. Both she and her cosmetics were a huge hit.

In 1955, Rose opened her second salon, the House of Beauty. Even though opening day was rainy and gray, over 10,000 women lined up to see the new salon. Rose worked hard to create a place where black women could go to be groomed and pampered. Her hard work paid off, and the House of Beauty made $200,000 in its first year.

In the 1940s and 50s, Rose's fashion shows drew huge crowds and rave reviews.

Accomplishments

1939 Opened the Rose Meta House of Beauty.

1940s Rose Meta House of Beauty became the largest black-owned beauty salon in the United States.

1955 Opened the House of Beauty which made $200,000 in its first year.

1972 Founded Trim-Away Figure Contouring.

Overcoming Obstacles

While Rose was growing up, she got a job working in a laundry. Sometimes her arms would get so tired from shaking out the sheets that she could barely move. She remembers complaining to her father who simply told her that she had made herself a "hard bed" and now she had to lie in it. From that time on, Rose decided not to have a "hard bed" all her life.

When Rose rented the run-down mansion which was to become the Rose Meta House of Beauty, most people told her that her venture was impossible. She had signed a ten-year lease but did not know if she would earn enough money to pay the rent. Also she did not know anything about renovation. But Rose remembered her father's advice to strive for success, and she refused to listen to her critics. She learned about renovating old houses, and soon the mansion was fixed up and remodeled into a beauty salon.

When Rose decided to open a second, more chic salon, she applied to the bank for a small loan. Although she had been doing business at this bank for twenty years, they refused to lend her the money. Rose did not let this stop her. She called up a different bank and was able to get a loan. With this and money she borrowed from friends and family, Rose opened up the House of Beauty. On its first day, the mayor's wife cut the ribbon at the opening celebrations.

Rose's success as a business person took its toll on her personal life. Building salons and training the workers took up most of her time. Rose married three times, but none of the marriages survived the pressures of her work. Rose's second husband was Joe Louis, the famous boxer. When they were dating, Joe asked Rose to stay and spend some time with him in Las Vegas. He expected Rose to jump at the offer, but Rose told him that she had to go back to New York to look after her salon. Joe was amazed and attracted by her devotion to her business. Rose and Joe married, but after a year and a half the marriage ended.

Rose has an excellent business sense, and for more than forty years she worked hard to make sure that her customers felt special.

Rose married former world champion heavyweight Joe Louis in December, 1955.

Special Interests

- Rose keeps in shape by working out on a walking machine seven days a week.
- Rose has used her business sense for other ventures. She helped form the Freedom National Bank in Harlem, and, in 1972, she founded a new business, Trim-Away Figure Contouring.

Naomi Sims

Personality Profile

Career: Successful model and business executive.

Born: March 30, 1949, in Oxford, Mississippi.

Family: Married Michael Findlay, 1973. Has one son, John Phillip.

Education: Westinghouse High School, Pittsburgh; the Fashion Institute of Technology in New York City.

Awards: Model of the Year, 1969, 1970; named a Woman of Achievement, *Ladies' Home Journal*, 1970; Board of Education Award, New York City; 1970; received key to the city of Cleveland, Ohio, 1971; International Best-Dressed List, 1971-1973, 1976, 1977; Modeling Hall of Fame International Mannequins, 1977.

Growing Up

Naomi had a lonely childhood. Her father divorced her mother when Naomi was just a baby. Today, she barely remembers what he looked like. Naomi's mother had a nervous breakdown in 1957, when Naomi was only eight. Naomi was separated from her two sisters, Betty and Doris, and sent to live in foster homes. She longed for the days when she could see her mother again, but it would never happen. Instead, Naomi was taken in by loving foster parents.

By the time Naomi was thirteen, she looked very different from the other teenagers. She was five-feet, ten-inches tall and appeared much older than her age. Many of her friends suggested she try modeling. After graduating from Westinghouse High School in Pittsburgh, Pennsylvania, she enrolled at the Fashion Institute of Technology in New York City.

Naomi did not have much money, so she decided to follow her friends' advice and try to find work as a model. First she posed for fashion drawings for six dollars an hour. Since she needed more money, Naomi called Gosta Peterson, a well-known fashion photographer, to see if he would hire her. Gosta felt Naomi had potential and agreed to help her. Soon Naomi was making sixty dollars an hour as a successful model.

Naomi's success comes directly from her interest in makeup and beauty.

Developing Skills

Naomi became the first African-American model to be featured on the cover of *Fashion of the Times*, a supplement to *The New York Times*. The photo helped break down the color barrier in the fashion industry. Naomi continued to prosper as a model. She appeared in AT & T commercials and was featured on the covers of such highly regarded magazines as *Vogue*, *Ladies' Home Journal*, *Life*, and *Cosmopolitan*. At age twenty-four, Naomi decided to leave modeling and go into business for herself.

Naomi's stunning good looks helped her rise to fame in the fashion industry.

Naomi began to manufacture and sell wigs. She wanted to develop wigs that would look good on African-American women. To make a wig that would have the same texture and color of black hair, Naomi invented a synthetic fiber. She formed her own company, the Naomi Sims Collection, and started visiting businesses that might sell her wigs. Soon her company became a financial success. In 1985, she founded Naomi Sims Beauty Products. Besides wigs, it produces a wide variety of beauty aids which are sold in department stores and specialty outlets across the United States and in the Bahamas.

As well, Naomi has developed a flair for writing. In 1975, she published her first book, *All about Health and Beauty for the Black Woman*. The book was a huge success, and Naomi published an updated version in 1986.

Naomi also wrote *How to Be a Top Model* (1979), *All about Hair Care for the Black Woman* (1982), and *All about Success for the Black Woman* (1983). She is also a regular contributor to *Right On!*, a national magazine that focuses on black teenagers.

As her business reputation grew, Naomi was asked to join several community organizations. She has been a participant in the Sickle-Cell Anemia Drive and the New York State Drug Rehabilitation Program. In 1980, Naomi was asked to be executive-in-residence for the School of Business Administration at Georgetown University in Washington, D.C. Four years later, she was a panel member of the Harvard Business School's career conference.

Naomi's books have become major beauty references for African-American women.

"I can't see myself modeling at thirty – it's too competitive and often shallow."

Accomplishments

1966 Enrolled at the Fashion Institute of Technology in New York City.

1967 First African-American woman to be featured on the cover of a major publication, *Fashion of the Times*.

1973 Ended modeling career and founded the Naomi Sims Collection.

1985 Founded Naomi Sims Beauty Products.

Overcoming Obstacles

As a child, Naomi often spent many hours by herself wishing for her natural mother to return. She was shuttled back and forth between foster families until one set of foster parents took her in as part of their family. Naomi felt that in order to succeed in the world, she would have to rely on herself.

Naomi was always interested in clothes, and at school she would often save her lunch money to buy earrings. Soon she realized that her height and interest in fashion were an advantage, and she decided to pursue a career in modeling. To launch her fashion career, she took an unheard-of gamble. She phoned a professional photographer and told him she wanted to be a model. Her gamble paid off.

"Once you've got success, it's empty. The fun is reaching for it."

But the early days were still difficult. Naomi faced periods of unemployment, and she often had to borrow money from her modeling agency. When her career finally started to take off, she had to drop out of college. It was difficult to be a full-time model and take classes at the same time.

In 1985, Naomi opened a number of stores to sell her products.

Although Naomi has found business success, it was a struggle at first. Many companies were uncertain if they should sell her products. Naomi used her reputation as a model to convince the stores to sell her wigs. She also put together a slide show which demonstrated her products and discussed the need for them. This approach usually succeeded, and many businesses agreed to represent her.

It is not easy to find the time to be a wife and mother when you are also a busy executive. But Naomi believes in the importance of spending time with her family. She often accompanies her husband, Michael Findlay, an art dealer, to shows across the country. They have one son, John Phillip. Naomi has tried her best to keep her private life away from media attention.

Special Interests

- Naomi is a busy lecturer. Not only does she speak about health and beauty, but also about drug abuse, sickle-cell anemia, and education.
- Naomi and her husband share an interest in art. Naomi collects the work of young American painters.
- Since Naomi had a difficult childhood, she is often concerned with the plight of young children. She is a member of the board of directors of the Northside Center Child Development in Harlem.

Madame C.J. Walker

Personality Profile

Career: Inventor of hair care products and founder of a successful beauty care business.

Born: 1867, in Delta, Louisiana, to Owen and Minerva Breedlove.

Died: May 25, 1919, in Irvington-on-Hudson, New York.

Family: Married Moses McWilliams, 1881, (died, 1887); married C.J. Walker, 1905. Had one daughter, Lelia.

Education: Learned to read and write with private tutors.

Awards: Inducted into National Women's Hall of Fame, 1993.

Growing Up

Known in her later life as Madame C.J. Walker, Sarah Breedlove was born in 1867 in Delta, Louisiana, the daughter of former slaves. Her childhood was one of great poverty and hardship. Every day she worked from sunrise to sunset in the cotton fields. Her family lived in a crumbling shack that had no windows and a dirt floor.

When she was seven, Sarah's parents died of yellow fever, and she was sent to live in Mississippi with her sister, Louvenia, and her brother-in-law. But Louvenia's husband showed young Sarah nothing but violent abuse. When she turned fourteen, Sarah escaped from his cruelty by marrying Moses McWilliams.

By the time she was seventeen, Sarah had given birth to her daughter, Lelia. At twenty, Sarah was widowed when Moses was killed by a lynch mob.

In 1887, Sarah and Lelia moved to St. Louis, Missouri, where her relatives helped Sarah find work washing clothes and cooking. With her meager earnings, Sarah supported herself and her daughter. She even saved enough money to send Lelia to school and college.

In the early 1900s, Madame C.J. Walker's Wonderful Hair Grower and Vegetable Shampoo sold for fifty cents each.

Sarah was very proud that, even though she was a poor, uneducated, black woman, she had still managed to give her daughter a college education.

Developing Skills

While living in St. Louis, Sarah began to have problems with baldness. At that time, black women were twisting their hair and wrapping it in string to straighten out the curls. This was very hard on the hair and, combined with a poor diet, usually resulted in hair loss.

Sarah experimented with different oils and shampoos. Using her own secret ingredients, she invented a product that not only stopped her hair loss, but also caused her hair to grow back. Amazed at the results, she tried it on her friends and family. They were delighted.

Sarah developed a hot comb to make hair styling easier and improved her Wonderful Hair Grower preparation. Then she started selling the preparation door-to-door.

In 1905, she moved to Denver with her sister-in-law and nieces. With only one dollar and fifty cents, Sarah began a hair products company. She asked for her family's help, and their attic soon became an assembly line where they filled jars with Wonderful Hair Grower.

An advertisement promoting Madame C.J. Walker's products.

"I am a woman who came from the cotton fields of the South. I was promoted from there to the washtub. Then I was promoted to the cook kitchen, and from there I PROMOTED MYSELF into the business of manufacturing hair goods and preparations."

The next year, Sarah married C.J. Walker, a newspaperman who knew a lot about advertising and mail-order sales. Learning from C.J.'s experience, Sarah began to sell the hair preparation through the mail and through a team of door-to-door sales people. As sales grew, she opened beauty parlors across the country. She also built her own factories and laboratories. In 1908, Sarah opened Lelia College in Pittsburgh to train women in the Walker method of hair grooming.

Sarah in front of her factory with her niece, factory director, and secretary.

Sarah continued to develop and expand her sales force of black women. By the time she died in 1919, over 25,000 women were Walker agents. Sarah was proud because she had given so many African-American women a chance to go into business and earn their own money.

Accomplishments

1905 Started her own company.

1906 Placed Lelia in charge of the mail-order operations.

1908 Opened Lelia College in Pittsburgh.

1910 Moved the company's headquarters to Indianapolis.

1913 Opened another Lelia College in New York. Was a presenter at the National Negro Business League convention.

1917 Sarah's company became the largest black-owned business in the United States.

Overcoming Obstacles

Although Sarah managed to overcome her poverty, she still had to deal with people who disagreed with her. Many in the black community felt that her hair straightening method was just a way for black women to imitate white women. They thought that Sarah was wrong to suggest that smooth, straight hair was better than coarse, curly hair. Even the churches got into the argument. The clergymen preached that if God had wanted blacks to have straight hair, he would have given it to them. Despite these protests, the demand for Sarah's products grew.

Sarah's ambition and hard work made her a millionaire. By 1917, her company was the largest black-owned business in the country with annual revenues of $500,000. But her success contributed to the breakup of her marriage. When the company's sales had reached ten dollars a week, Sarah's husband told her that she should be satisfied. He tried to persuade her to slow down. The marriage ended because of their business disagreements.

With her new wealth, Sarah built a house for herself by the Hudson River in Irvington, New York.

Back then, white people always called black women by their first names. To avoid this and gain more respect for herself in the community, Sarah kept the name Madame C.J. Walker.

There were many people who would not recognize Sarah's success because she was a woman. In 1912, Sarah attended a convention of the National Negro Business League. The chairman tried to stop her from speaking, but Sarah walked calmly to the podium and gave a speech to the convention. At the end of her speech, the hall was filled with applause. The next year, Sarah was invited to be a presenter at the convention.

One of the greatest difficulties that Sarah overcame was her illiteracy. As the daughter of former slaves, she had no chance to go to school. Later, when she was a success, she hired tutors to teach her to read and write, and lawyers to help her with her business. During the first years of her business, she signed all her bank papers with a scrawl. As she learned to read and write, her handwriting improved so much that the bank called to make sure that the new signature was really her own.

Sarah with Booker T. Washington and other members of the National Negro Business League.

Special Interests

- Sarah put great emphasis on education and donated thousands of dollars to schools and institutes in Florida, Georgia, and North Carolina.
- Sarah never forgot the poverty and racism of her early years. She supported causes such as Monroe Trotter's National Equal Rights League and the NAACP's anti-lynching drive. In 1917, she marched from Harlem to the White House with other black leaders to confront President Wilson about anti-lynching laws.

Oprah Winfrey

Personality Profile

Career: Talk-show host, actor, and owner of a television and film production company.

Born: January 29, 1954, in Kosciusko, Mississippi, to Vernon Winfrey and Vernita Lee.

Education: East High School; Tennessee State University.

Awards: Miss Fire Prevention, Nashville, 1971; Miss Black Tennessee, 1971; Nominated for Academy Award and Golden Globe Award for best supporting actress for role of Sophia in *The Color Purple,* 1986; Women of Achievement Award, National Organization for Women, 1986; Broadcaster of the Year Award, International Radio and Television Society, 1988; Entertainer of the Year Award, NAACP, 1989, three Daytime Emmy awards for the *Oprah Winfrey Show,* 1989.

Growing Up

Even as a small child, Oprah showed she had many talents. She made her first public speech at age three in the local church. In kindergarten, she wrote a letter asking her teacher to move her to the first grade. It happened the next day.

Until she was six, Oprah was raised by her grandmother. Later she moved to Milwaukee, Wisconsin, to live with her mother, a housecleaner. Her mother's long work hours made it difficult for her to give Oprah the attention she needed. These years were difficult for Oprah, and she had many problems. In 1968, at fourteen, she went to live with her father in Nashville.

Her father, Vernon, and his wife, Zelma, were respected members of the community. Vernon was a barber, grocery store owner, city councillor, and church deacon. He made Oprah give up her make-up, revealing clothes, and bad attitude. He encouraged her to read and do well in school. Every two weeks, he asked her to prepare five book reports on books she had chosen from the library.

Vernon and Zelma's influence on Oprah began to take effect. She was chosen to attend the White House Youth Conference in 1970. She knew that she wanted to go to college and study performing arts. She won a $1,000 scholarship for her speech "The Negro, the Constitution, and the United States" and enrolled at Tennessee State University.

Oprah's mother wanted to name her Orpah, from the book of Ruth in the Bible. But someone misspelled the name on her birth certicate by switching the 'p' and 'r' and she became known as Oprah.

Developing Skills

When Oprah was seventeen, she got a job as a part-time newscaster on a local radio station. In 1973, while still attending Tennessee State University, Oprah was hired as a reporter and news anchor at WTVF-TV in Nashville.

Oprah worked at WJZ-TV in Baltimore, Maryland, from 1976 to 1983. She started as an anchor but was not ready for the position and was fired. But the station had a contract with Oprah, so they asked her to cohost a morning talk show, "People Are Talking." The ratings soon rose.

In 1987, Oprah hosted a benefit for Passages Inc., a group that helps women enter the workforce.

In 1984, Oprah received an offer to host "A.M. Chicago." The show was aired at the same time as the top-ranked "Phil Donahue Show." Oprah began to study improvisation with the Second City comedy troupe to polish her entertainment skills. Oprah's show took off and soon topped Donahue in the ratings. It was shown in more than 120 American cities.

The next year, Oprah was noticed by movie producer Quincy Jones. He asked her to audition for the role of Sophia in his upcoming movie *The Color Purple*. Oprah won the part and was nominated for a Golden Globe and an Academy Award for best supporting actress.

"The Oprah Winfrey Show" made its national debut in September, 1986. It became an immediate success. Seventeen million people watch her show in 192 cities. It is one of the highest-ranked shows in syndication, and Oprah became the highest-paid performer in show business.

In addition to forming her own television production company, Harpo Productions (Oprah spelled backwards), Oprah expanded into other businesses. She is the part-owner of three television stations and a Chicago restaurant called The Eccentric.

Oprah has many plans that will keep her busy in the future. She owns the film rights to *Beloved*, a story of slavery by Toni Morrison, and intends to play the lead role. Oprah also owns the screen rights to *Their Eyes Were Watching God*, a novel by Zora Neale Hurston. Oprah's work as a public speaker and fund raiser round out her busy schedule.

In 1994, Oprah won a Daytime Emmy award for "The Oprah Winfrey Show."

Accomplishments

1973 Reporter and anchor for WTVF-TV in Nashville.	**1987** Acted in *Native Son*.
1976-77 News anchor for WJZ-TV in Baltimore, Maryland.	**1988** Established Harpo Productions and assumed ownership of "The Oprah Winfrey Show."
1984 Host of "A.M. Chicago."	**1989** Co-produced and starred in the miniseries *The Women of Brewster Place*.
1985 Acted in *The Color Purple*.	
1986 "A.M. Chicago" became nationally syndicated as "The Oprah Winfrey Show."	**1990** Starred in the weekly television show "The Women of Brewster Place."

Overcoming Obstacles

Oprah is a perfect example of the American "rags-to-riches" story. She was born to a teenage mother, and her father did not even know she had been born until he received a birth announcement in the mail with a note that said, "Send clothes."

In 1988, Oprah showed off her weight loss on her television show.

Although Oprah's early years with her grandmother were happy, that all changed when she moved to Milwaukee to be with her mother. Oprah made up stories to get her mother's attention. Once she even staged a fake robbery at her home to get new glasses. She claimed that the "thieves" knocked her unconscious and broke her glasses.

The most difficult time of Oprah's life was between the ages of nine and fourteen. A teenaged cousin and several other male relatives and friends sexually abused her. Through these difficult years, Oprah found her refuge in books. She talked about the abuse on her show in 1991, hoping to help others who had been abused.

"My father turned my life around by insisting that I be more than I was and by believing I could be more. His love of learning showed me the way."

When she began to work for television, Oprah's producers felt that her looks were not right for her show "People Are Talking." They thought her eyes were too far apart, her nose too wide, and her chin too long. When the station wanted her to thin her hair, she had a permanent. This was a mistake, and she was temporarily bald. She vowed never again to let herself be controlled by executives.

Oprah's concern for others and her bright personality have helped her show become a success.

Oprah's most famous problem has been her weight. When she finished making "People Are Talking," she weighed 160 pounds, but she soon began to gain weight. She lost much of that when she went on a liquid diet but soon put back many of the lost pounds. She started a new program to keep the weight off, and this has proven more successful. Oprah admits that her weight problems result from using food to relieve stress.

Special Interests

- Oprah has established a "Little Sisters" program in Chicago's Cabrini-Green housing project to give counselling and help to young girls.
- She is involved in helping child abuse victims. She lobbies to keep nationwide records on convicted child abusers, and for new laws for strict sentencing of people convicted of child abuse.
- Oprah set up a $750,000 fund to provide ten scholarships each year at her college. She sends letters to each scholarship winner.

Don Cornelius

Don took a broadcasting course and, in 1966, got a part-time job at WVON Radio in Chicago.

Don married young and spent the next few years trying to find enough money to pay the bills. He sold tires, cars, and insurance to support his family. Because he had a great voice, friends suggested he would make a good radio announcer.

Don took a broadcasting course and, in 1966, got a part-time job at WVON Radio in Chicago. The pay was poor, but Don enjoyed the job. He worked in the news department and as a late-night disc jockey. He also did talk shows, commercials, and public affairs programs.

Don became friends with Roy Wood at the station, and when Roy joined WCIU-TV, Don started working part-time at the television station.

Don had an idea for a new show, "Soul Train." Similar to Dick Clark's "American Bandstand," "Soul Train" would feature teenagers singing and dancing to popular black music. He presented his idea to the station's managers, and they agreed to give him a chance.

Finding sponsors for the show was much more difficult. Don ran into several dead ends. Finally he met George O'Hara, a manager at Sears, Roebuck & Co., who offered to help. "Soul Train" was first shown on August 17, 1970, and soon became Chicago's Number One show among African Americans.

The show kept Don busy. He hosted, produced, and sold all the advertising for "Soul Train." It was difficult at first to find other sponsors, but Don persevered. In the months that followed, more and more big-name advertisers signed on board.

Personality Profile

Career: Created "Soul Train," the longest-running black music show in television history. Has also sponsored music and entertainment awards for African Americans.

Born: September 27, 1936, in Chicago, Illinois.

Education: DuSable High School, Chicago; attended broadcasting school, 1966.

"Soul Train" went national on October 2, 1971. However, only seven of the twenty-five stations that Don felt would broadcast the show actually did. Despite this setback, ratings soared. After eight months, all twenty-five stations aired the show. In August, 1972, Don signed a million-dollar advertising deal with Johnson Products. This company, owned by African-American George Johnson, manufactured hair and facial products for young blacks, the same people who composed most of "Soul Train's" audience.

After the success of "Soul Train," Don decided to form Soul Train Records in 1975 with Dick Griffey, who also worked for the show. Soul Train Records released only twelve albums a year which were distributed by RCA. After three years, the company dissolved so Don and Dick could work on other projects.

Don's work with "Soul Train" continued smoothly until December, 1982, when he was rushed to the hospital for brain surgery. Don underwent a twenty-one hour operation. He recovered and missed only the next six months of "Soul Train."

In 1986, he launched the "Soul Train Music Awards," the only music awards show dedicated to black musicians. By 1992, "Soul Train" had become the longest-running black music show in television history. The following year, Don started the "Soul Train Comedy Awards" to honor black comedians.

Accomplishments

1970 "Soul Train" began on WCIU-TV.

1971 "Soul Train" became a nationally syndicated program. It was broadcast on seven stations.

1972 "Soul Train" expanded its broadcast to twenty-five stations. Don signed an advertising deal with Johnson Products.

1986 Launched the "Soul Train Music Awards."

1993 Launched the "Soul Train Comedy Awards."

Patrick Kelly

At the age of six, Patrick knew he wanted to be in the fashion business. While flipping through his grandmother's magazines, he discovered there were no black models. He decided to create fashions for black women. Even before he started high school, Patrick was designing dance and prom gowns for the girls in his area. Later he designed department store window displays. He also did sketches for the stores' newspaper advertisements.

In 1972, Patrick enrolled in art history and African-American history classes at Jackson State University. He quickly became bored and longed to be part of the fashion industry. Patrick moved to Atlanta, Georgia, where he sorted clothing for AMVETS, an American veterans' association. He realized AMVETS had a large collection of designer clothing. He decided to open his own antique clothing store with some of these items. He also designed and sewed clothes and sold them on the street. To get more experience, he decorated windows for free at the Yves Saint Laurent boutique. The management realized how talented he was and gave him a small salary. During this time, he met Pat Cleveland, a fashion model, who encouraged him to seek greater opportunities in New York.

Personality Profile

Career: One of the world's leading fashion designers.

Born: September 24, 1954, in Vicksburg, Mississippi, to Danie and Letha Kelly.

Died: January 1, 1990, in Paris, France.

Education: Vicksburg Senior High School; Jackson State University; Parsons School of Design.

Awards: Member of the *Chambre Syndicale du Prêt-à-Porter*, 1988.

Patrick took her advice and enrolled in New York's Parsons School of Design. He supported himself by making dresses to sell to models. At the time he finished his course, jobs in the fashion industry were scarce. Pat Cleveland suggested he go to France, but Patrick said he could not afford to go. The next day he received a one-way plane ticket to Paris in an envelope that had no return address.

Patrick discovered his true potential in Paris. He worked as a clothing designer for the night club Le Palace. He also sewed clothes and sold them on the streets, slowly building a strong customer base. In 1984, an exclusive Paris boutique, Victorie, bought his dresses and gave him a workroom and showroom of his own.

Patrick became friends with Bjorn Amelan, a photographer's agent. They formed a new company, Patrick Kelly Paris. Through Bjorn's connections, Patrick was able to display his designs to a wider audience.

In June, 1987, Patrick met and impressed Linda Wachner, the chief executive officer of Warnaco, a clothing manufacturer. They signed a multimillion-dollar contract, and Warnaco created a special Kelly line of clothing. Patrick became the first American to display his own designs in Paris fashion shows.

In 1988, Patrick was invited to become a member of the *Chambre Syndicale du Prêt-à-Porter*, an exclusive fashion designers' club. His work was displayed in such highly regarded places as the Louvre Palace in Paris.

Patrick's days at the top of the fashion industry were cut short when he contracted bone marrow disease and died on January 1, 1990. He was only thirty-six years old.

Accomplishments

1974 Opened his own antique-clothing store and began selling his own designs.

1979 Arrived in Paris and got a job his first day there.

1984 Unveiled his famous black tube dress and obtained workshop and showroom space in the Victorie boutique.

1986-87 Received a number of freelance contracts to design clothing for companies such as Benetton. Sold the world-wide rights to his women's ready-to-wear line to Warnaco.

1988 Invited to become a member of the *Chambre Syndicale du Prêt-à-Porter*.

Ernesta Procope

E rnesta was born in Brooklyn, New York, the only daughter of West Indian immigrants, Clarence and Elvira. Ernesta loved music and began taking piano lessons when she was eight. When she was thirteen, she and eight other students were featured in a concert at Carnegie Hall.

Ernesta continued her music studies until she met and married Albin Bowman, a Brooklyn real-estate developer. Albin owned many properties in low-income neighborhoods but had trouble getting insurance for them. He decided to insure the properties himself and wanted Ernesta to help him. He encouraged her to enrol at the Pohs Institute of Insurance.

Ernesta graduated from the Institute in 1950 and began handling Albin's insurance accounts. By the time Albin died in 1952, she was looking after all his insurance needs. In 1953, she started the E.G. Bowman Company which helped black people get insurance from other companies for their properties. That same year, she married John Procope.

In the late 1960s, riots began breaking out in some sections of Brooklyn. The insurance companies were afraid that they would lose money if a lot of properties were damaged and the owners filed claims. The companies started canceling the policies of Ernesta's clients, leaving them without any insurance. Ernesta told the governor of New York about the problem that black home owners were facing. Hearings were held, and the New York State Fair Plan was passed. The plan guaranteed home owners' insurance in low-income neighborhoods.

Ernesta realized that her company needed to grow. In 1970, she began to look after the insurance needs of businesses. Ernesta stressed the importance of on-the-job safety, reducing insurance costs, and analyzing health and safety risks. Within a short time, she had signed up clients such as IBM, PepsiCo., General Motors, Avon Products, and Time Warner.

Personality Profile

Career: Founder and president of the nation's largest black-owned insurance agency.

Born: In Brooklyn, New York, to Clarence and Elvira Foster.

Education: New York High School of Music and Art; Brooklyn College; Pohs Institute of Insurance.

Awards: Woman of the Year, *Tuesday Magazine*, 1972; Business Achievement Award, National Business League, 1976; Entrepreneur of the Year, Northeastern Region of the U.S. Commerce Department, 1987; Distinguished Service Award, NAACP, 1991; Entrepreneurial Excellence Award, DowJones/*Wall Street Journal*, 1992; Lifetime Achievement Award, 1993; and many honorary degrees.

She also got the contract to insure the employees of the Community Development Agency, a New York organization which fights poverty. Ernesta formed Bowman-Procope Associates to look after the CDA benefit programs.

Because of her knowledge of how corporations work and her excellent people skills, Ernesta has been invited to join the board of directors of corporations such as Avon Products, the Salvation Army, Chubb Corporation, and Urban National Corporation.

Ernesta has continued to provide insurance for homes, churches, and schools such as Howard University. She believes in the importance of giving good service to all her clients, whether they are multimillion-dollar companies or simply home owners.

Ernesta likes to help out other women and encourages them to enter the insurance business. Her staff are mostly women.

Accomplishments

1950	Obtained her real estate licence.
1953	Formed the E.G. Bowman Company.
1970	Obtained E.G. Bowman's first corporate client and formed Bowman-Procope Associates.
1993	Elected Chair of Adelphi University.

Barbara Gardner Proctor

Since her mother was a young, single parent, Barbara was raised by her grandmother and uncle in Black Mountain, North Carolina. Barbara earned high marks in school and received a scholarship to Talladega College in Alabama where she earned degrees in education and psychology.

After graduating from college, Barbara worked for the summer at a children's camp in Michigan. She planned to return to North Carolina in the fall and teach, but she had only enough money to get to Chicago. A friend got her a job writing commentary on record jackets. In 1958, she became the jazz music critic and an editor of *Down Beat*. Later she worked for Vee-Jay Records International, writing reviews for the covers of jazz record albums. She rose to become international director of the company.

Barbara earned high marks in school and received a scholarship to Talladega College in Alabama where she earned degrees in education and psychology.

In 1960, Barbara married Carl Proctor. Carl worked in the music industry managing singers' careers, and for a while Barbara worked with him. When the marriage ended, Barbara decided to go into advertising. She got a job with a Chicago advertising agency and began by writing Pine Sol labels.

Barbara's biggest setbacks may have led to her success. She worked at an agency that made a television commercial which imitated civil rights demonstrations. It showed a group of housewives running down the street, waving cans, and demanding that hairdressers foam their hair. Barbara hated the commercial. She felt it made fun of the civil rights movement and women. When she refused to work on the account, she lost her job.

Barbara decided to get a loan from the Small Business Administration to start her own advertising agency. She borrowed enough money to get the company started, and, in 1971, Barbara founded Proctor & Gardner Advertising.

Barbara had two strikes against her when she started her company — she was black and female. At that time, most of the advertising agencies were run by white men. In order to get respect for her own company, Barbara named her firm Proctor & Gardner Advertising. Many people thought that Gardner was a man who stayed at the office and ran the agency. They respected the company because they believed that a man was in charge. In reality, there never was a Gardner. Barbara was both people.

Personality Profile

Career: Owner of one the country's most successful advertising agencies.

Born: November 30, 1933, in Black Mountain, North Carolina, the only child of single mother, Bernice.

Education: Talladega College, B.A.s in education and psychology.

Awards: Frederick Douglass Humanitarian Award, 1975; American TV Commercial awards; Blackbook Businesswoman of the Year, 1974-75; Chicago Advertising Woman of the Year, 1974-75; Small Business of the Year Award, 1978; Black Media Award for Outstanding Professional, 1980; "Hero of the '80s" from President Ronald Reagan, 1987; many honorary degrees.

The early days of the company were hard. Barbara had a tiny office above a restaurant, and her young son slept in the office while she worked. But she believed that an agency looking after the needs of minorities could succeed. After several years, many well-known firms became her clients.

Barbara chose not to work with companies that exploited minorities and women. She also disliked drug, tobacco, and alcohol companies because she felt that they were partly responsible for the growing alcohol, drug, and smoking problems. Her firm still refuses to accept these accounts.

Her business success and community work have been recognized. Barbara was named "Hero of the '80s" by President Ronald Reagan and has received many honors including the well-known Clio Award from the American Television Commercial Festival. Barbara has also been given honorary degrees from many colleges and universities.

Accomplishments

1958 Became jazz music critic and contributing editor of *Down Beat*.

1961-64 Employed by Vee-Jay Records, eventually became international director.

1965-68 Employed by Post-Keys-Gardner Advertising.

1968-69 Employed by Gene Taylor Associates.

1969-70 Worked as a copy supervisor for North Advertising Agency.

1971 Founded her own agency, Proctor & Gardner Advertising.

1978-82 Served as president of the League of Black Women.

Susan Taylor

Susan never intended to become a writer.

As editor-in-chief of *Essence*, a magazine about African-American women, Susan has met some of the world's most interesting black people. She has interviewed talk-show host and business executive Oprah Winfrey, and has spoken with Winnie Mandela, a South African leader. Susan has been with the magazine since it began in 1970, and as the magazine has grown, so have Susan's responsibilities. She is presently a vice-president of the company which owns *Essence*.

Susan never intended to become a writer. Instead, she wanted to be a beautician and first became interested in beauty while growing up in Harlem, New York. She spent much of her spare time reading fashion and beauty magazines, and, after graduating from high school, Susan took a course in cosmetology.

Even though she had never taken a writing course, Susan decided that she wanted to write about beauty. In 1970, she contacted *Essence*, which was just starting up as a magazine especially for black women and was looking for free-lance writers. She wrote articles for the beauty section, and the editors liked her writing style so much that the next year, when they needed a full-time beauty editor, they hired Susan. The company could not afford to pay her much, and Susan struggled to pay her bills. As a single mother, she found it difficult to juggle her career and home life. At times Susan felt like quitting. She discussed her problem with a minister who told Susan that she had to believe in herself. Hoping that she would get promoted and make more money, Susan decided to stay at *Essence*.

Susan's hard work and determination paid off. She took on new duties and became responsible for the fashion sections as well as the beauty articles. When she was thirty-five, Susan became editor-in-chief of *Essence*.

As the editor-in-chief, Susan has led the magazine in new directions. Her reporters cover such stories as drug abuse and crime, and, although she is busy directing the reporters, Susan still writes for the magazine. In a column titled "In the Spirit," she writes about many topics, always stressing the importance of taking pride in one's accomplishments.

Personality Profile

Career: Editor and television host.

Born: January 23, 1946, in New York, New York.

Education: B.A., Fordham University, 1990.

Awards: Women in Communications Matrix Award; honorary Doctorate of Humane Letters, Lincoln University, 1988; many other awards.

Essence has grown under Susan's leadership. When it started in 1970, it had a small readership. It now has fifty thousand readers and makes more than twenty million dollars a year. That growth in popularity encouraged the owners of the magazine to move *Essence* into television. They wanted to produce a television show which dealt with the same kinds of topics as the magazine. In 1986, Susan was asked to produce and host the show.

This was a very busy time for Susan. As well as editing the magazine and hosting and producing the television show, she also took classes at Fordham University in New York City. In 1990, she received a degree in social science and economics. That same year, the television show ended.

Susan still keeps busy. She is a member of several journalism clubs and supports many women's organizations. Since her family did not have much money when she was growing up, Susan understands the problems that low-income people face and works to help them. She also understands the obstacles single mothers must overcome and encourages them to take charge of their lives.

Accomplishments

1970 Free-lance writer for *Essence*.

1971 Promoted to *Essence* beauty editor.

1972 Became *Essence* beauty and fashion editor.

1981 Named *Essence* editor-in-chief.

1986 Named vice-president of Essence Communications; produced and hosted "The Essence Television Show."

Maggie L. Walker

Maggie had to work hard at an early age. Her father was murdered when she was a child. With bills piling high, Maggie's mother worked overtime doing others' laundry. Maggie carried the laundry back and forth for her mother's clients and looked after her brother.

In 1881, at fourteen, Maggie joined the Independent Order of Saint Luke (IOSL) in Richmond, Virginia. The organization was created after the Civil War to help blacks bury the dead and assist the sick. Maggie loved the IOSL and believed in its goals of self-help and cooperation among black people. She quickly gained greater responsibility in the IOSL, eventually becoming Right Worthy Grand Secretary in 1899.

Maggie had her work cut out for her. The IOSL only had $31.61 in the bank and a stack of bills to pay. Her sharp management pulled the organization around. In 1904, she decided the IOSL needed its own bank. Black people could use the bank to save money and to get loans to pay for their own homes. That same year, her dream came true, and Saint Luke's Penny Thrift Savings Bank opened. Maggie became its first president – the first woman bank president in the United States.

The bank played a major role in the lives of African-American families. Children were given small boxes to save their pennies, and, with one dollar, they could open a savings account. Parents were helped through savings and loan programs. By 1920, 645 homes for black families had been bought with loans from the bank. The bank still exists as the Consolidated Bank and Trust Company.

Besides her work at the bank and the IOSL, Maggie worked tirelessly for the community. She helped a community house get started, she supported a tuberculosis hospital for black people, and she served on many associations working to improve conditions for African Americans.

Maggie also started a newspaper, *The St. Luke Herald*. The first issue of this weekly paper was published on March 29, 1902. The paper looked at black issues and had many articles about civil rights. It also contained a special children's section which printed letters from children across the country. For thirty years, Maggie was the newspaper's editor.

Personality Profile

Career: Founded a bank and served as its president. Was also active in community affairs, civil rights, and feminism.

Born: July 15, 1867, in Richmond, Virginia.

Died: December 15, 1934, in Richmond, Virginia.

Education: Armstrong Normal and High School, 1883.

In 1907, Maggie fell on the front steps of her home and badly injured her knees. By the 1920s, the pain forced her to spend much of her time in an upstairs room or on the glassed-in front porch. But Maggie was not lonely. She was held in such high regard in the community that people often stopped by the porch to visit with her and exchange the news of the day. Despite her injury, she remained editor of *The St. Luke Herald* and president of the bank.

Maggie was very close to her family, and she renovated her house so they could all live together. But Maggie suffered personal tragedy in 1915 when her son mistook her husband for a prowler and killed him. Maggie stood by her son throughout his trial. He was eventually acquitted.

Maggie retired from the bank in 1932 but stayed on as chairman of the board. When she died two years later, the entire community mourned. Her funeral service was one of the largest in Richmond's history. Maggie's house still stands today and has been named a national historic landmark.

Accomplishments

1890 The Magdelena Council, Number 125, of the IOSL was named in honor of Maggie.

1899 Named the Right Worthy Grand Secretary of the IOSL.

1902 Established *The St. Luke Herald.*

1904 Persuaded the IOSL to establish a bank, now called the Consolidated Bank and Trust Company.

Index

1 2 3 4 5 6 7 8 9 0 Printed in Canada 4 3 2 1 0 9 8 7 6 5